D0911036

THE SENTINEL

THE SENTINEL

A. F. MORITZ

Poems

ANANSI

Published in 2008 by
House of Anansi Press Inc.
110 Spadina Avenue, Suite 801
Toronto, ON, M5V 2K4
Tel. 416-363-4343
Fax 416-363-1017
www.anansi.ca

Distributed in Canada by
HarperCollins Canada Ltd.
1995 Markham Road
Scarborough, ON, M1B 5M8
Toll free tel. 1-800-387-0117

Distributed in the United States by
Publishers Group West
1700 Fourth Street
Berkeley, CA, 94710
Toll free tel. 1-800-788-3123

14 13 12 11 10   3 4 5 6 7

Library and Archives Canada Cataloguing in Publication

Moritz, A. F.
The sentinel / A.F. Moritz.

Poems.
ISBN 978-0-88784-790-5

I. Title.

PS8576.O724S46 2008   C811'.54   C2007-907082-5

Library of Congress Control Number: 2007940447

Cover design: Bill Douglas at The Bang
Text design and typesetting: Ingrid Paulson

  Canada Council   Conseil des Arts    ONTARIO ARTS COUNCIL
         for the Arts   du Canada   CONSEIL DES ARTS DE L'ONTARIO

*We acknowledge for their financial support of our publishing program the
Canada Council for the Arts, the Ontario Arts Council, and the
Government of Canada through the Canada Book Fund.*

Printed and bound in Canada

Contents

The Butterfly

That day I remember when the butterfly
was expected, the whole city flooded down
to the harbour to wait and welcome, crowding
everywhere on the burnt, blackened wharves,
the crumbled docks and piers, climbing and fighting
to find a place from which the ocean, spread like a bat wing,
and the horizon could be seen. Toward noon
it appeared, a watered pink at first, a fleck
as of blood in saliva, fluttering crazily,
seeming not even to make toward us—and yet
it came on swiftly, spreading and rising up all at once,
a roaring orange veined with black, and blotted out
the sun. Between those fiery curtains, each
a hemisphere, the tube of worm was like
some cylindrical ship of living metal
where beings who had travelled from the stars
for centuries would peer out through ports
of black crystal…except that they were dead inside
and the sweet rot smell of carelessly preserved
entomological specimens filled the light.
Soon, though, it changed again, to Mourning Cloak,
to Tiger Swallowtail, to a humble yellow thing
that brought its own garden roiling under it
to replace the coal-tar waves. The sea was all spiked flowers,
goldenrod, lupin, loosestrife, delphinium,
and the butterfly stopped its anabasis our way
and got lost in the colours. We saw it hovering,
going on, nearer, farther, so frantic mad
with always more delight it could not pause
on any single crown. And then its female

came to it out of nowhere and the two tied a knot
in the air, and he stabbed his body into hers clinging
to a green translucent stem. A sparrow next,
a bird larger than an Africa of cloud
and yet demonically light and agile,
when they took flight, ate one of them
after a brief arabesque of dogfight. Was it our fly
that still lived? Then the hurricane—a little breeze that rose
when a spot darkened the sun—drove it tumbling
into the leaves. Torn petals
crowded the atmosphere, and whether its wings
of taut anile skin had been shattered and blown
with the flower fragments, or it had survived,
we couldn't see. It had dived like a fighter jet
going down into the jungle, hit,
behind a hill from which a moment later
comes up a plume of flame, but not a flame,
a burst of quiet came. And then our wait
seemed gone and we were watching
the black ocean again, congealed and trembling.

BETTER DAYS

YOUR STORY

Remember that you once lived, that you were,
that you were someplace here (I almost added
"with us in our world" but that might not be so).
Remember you had a story, even if you never knew.
Someone saw or felt you
and had to decide, had to make up
a history of you, even if it was a lie:
that you were nothing and easily forgotten.
And so you were, and it was too,
he forgot, we all forgot you, and now
nobody knows that story that is always being
rewritten: just as it meant
to do, it vanished with you. Even if
the perfect police erased you, knocked at your
navel or sex or the space between
with ceramic knuckle and wooden stock and slammed
through your flimsy door and scraped you
from your bed, and took you
and so you were warehoused—small
change of bones—with crawfish claws and mouse teeth
nowhere but in my charnel would-be
carnal words, nevertheless
remember. Even as I
command you this, I know
you don't. There's nothing to remember
and no one to remember it except
all of you unknown equally
in my voice or anywhere.

PLACE

A place belongs to the one who has most deeply
loved it, they said, has hoped in it beyond
its self-corruption. The land, people, the city

is his if his nights are for recalling it,
calling it in tears of aloneness and amazed
thanksgiving: that luck let him kiss it in his childhood,

that it grew into him, is him, that he still wants
to have it, save it, he wonders what it knows
tonight, right now, how it is with that place,

if it's happy, dying, dead. So he went back
carrying his book of that city: a great book,
yet only a dim sketch of his memory,

though in its pages, closed and dark, the alleys
of cracked windows and lintels, and children's paths
through towering weeds behind the empty stores

and under sycamores down to the river, burn
with bright emptiness that in the city were full of dust,
discarded bottles, concrete crumbs, and rusted

shavings in broken light. He did not have
a dollar in that place. He could not find
a door to open. He did not know a soul.

WARREN

Look at this place again: vast, splendid, even lush, a forest city,
with refreshing green softening the human materials and angles,
with wind in the leaves a constant washing of clean water,
dark or bright. And it's true, the little city we came from long ago
was a squalid failure: every part of it half-used and spoiled,
tumbled on itself, blocking up its own nostrils, pores, and bowels,
crushing its own hands and head. As if, after furious but moronic
labour for a century, it had managed only to make its own body
a smoky, narrow warren where it hid three-quarters dead
in the vomit and filth it emitted. But we were smart and shining
and we came here. What are we, who have lain inside that den
and through a mossy hole have glimpsed this moon we see now
float free over silver towers? And the people that we found here:
do they purr like the best engines and glint all of the time
like the sun off chrome because within them they don't have
any black dirty burrow or any space where one once was?

Better Days

Never anymore in a wash of sweetness and awe
does the summer I was seventeen come back
to mind against my will, like a bird crossing

my vision. Summer of moist nights full of girls
and boys ripened, holy drunkenness and violation
of the comic boundaries, defiances that never

failed or brought disaster. Days on the backs
and in the breath of horses, between rivers
and pools that reflected the cicadas' whine,

enervation and strength creeping in smooth waves
over muscular water. All those things accepted,
once, with unnoticing hunger, as an infant

accepts the nipple, never come back to mind
against the will. What comes unsummoned now,
blotting out every other thought and image,

is a part of the past not so deep or far away:
the time of poverty, of struggle to find means
not hateful—the muddy seedtime of early manhood.

What returns are those moments in the diner
night after night with each night's one cup of coffee,
watching an old man, who always at the same hour

came in and smiled, ordered a tea and opened
his drawing pad. What did he fill it with?
And where's he gone? Those days, that studious worker,

hand moving and eyes eager in the sour light,
that artist always in the same worn-out suit,
are my nostalgia now. That old man comes back,

the friend I saw each day and never spoke to,
because I hoped soon to disappear from there,
as I have disappeared, into the heaven of better days.

What Way

At the table, at the grave not knowing
whether to grieve or celebrate, they seemed
to find a way within the stalled noon clatter
and the dusk over oily swamps and elder tangle
along a locked stockade of heavy machines,
as the blue heron, looking down, flew farther on.
Nothing dissolved for them the mortal green
and black in transparent power of spacious streams
now gone from earth. The flickering they found,
terror-hope-terror, in fire of sunset clouds
remained unwavering in its progress to night
and day and night. And yet the pleasure they took
in everything did not wear out. The limestone
quarry of a poorer century, lipped in birds
and berries, treasured up, still treasures up,
old rains beneath its surface of dusty jet—
still waits behind their houses on airless nights
to be the dreams and drownings of new children.

You That I Loved

You that I loved all my life long,
you are not the one.
You that I followed, my line or path or way,
that I followed singing, and you
earth and air of the world the way went through,
and you who stood around it so it could be
the way, you forests and cities,
you deer and opossums struck by the lonely hunter
and left decaying, you paralyzed obese ones
who sat on a falling porch in a deep green holler
and observed me, your bald dog barking,
as I stumbled past in a hurry along my line,
you are not the one. But you
are the one, you that I loved all my life long,
you I still love so in my dying mind
I grasp me loving you when we are gone.
You are the one, you path or way or line
that winds beside the house where she and I live on,
still longing though long gone
for the health of all forests and cities,
and one day to visit them,
one day be rich and free enough to go and see
the restricted wonders of the earth.
ʼAnd you are the one, old ladies fated from birth
to ugliness, obesity and dearth,
who sat beside my path
one day as I flashed by. And you are the one,
all tumble-down shacks in disregarded hills
and animals the car on the road kills
and leaves stinking in the sun.

Happiness of Wandering

Happiness of wandering, it's you who are
with me when I've fallen asleep, or is it
when I've woken up, and my lost love is here.

There's a light bulb in a cage over a steel door.

She's wearing a really sharp short-skirted suit,
maroon set off with a few thin violet stripes,
and she tells me she's finished, let's go somewhere and talk.

Dawn over a red clay field of ruts.
The world-long rose-blue steps of the sky are of course empty.

Now she's sitting. Her body, where it folds,
dreams farther on: to endlessness as mature as a road
that curves behind the hills, followed for ages.

Twigs of a December bush: map with no legend.
There's a pair of panties, cheap nylon, lying on the slag.
A naked woman on a card between two winter oak leaves.

And now she gets up. I can't remember what we say
or where we go, and I hate memory but I remember
her grin in profile, her lashes from above.

Take note: enclosed stairway where one could sleep.
Six big men in the car, with knives and bats.
Humidity swallows breath at the turn-off to Mars Hill.
No rest on Basin Street above a thumping bar.

Was this when I told her my theory about home?
We've tried dwelling where we were born, I said,
and finding where we belong, and look: neither one works.

A full moon over the highway into Richmond, Indiana.
The driver claims he wrote the Dickey Lee hit, "Patches."
Sparks reel from chrome scraping the bridge rails.
A hurricane-lifted cabin cruiser in the trees near Ponchartrain.
Swimmer naked and deserted as the surf.

Only in wandering do you pass lamps and doors
where people are truly at home, sleeping not dying,
where life is the health you're after, but not if you stop.

There's a Luger under the seat, he says. Heft it.
Goldenrod out the windshield.
A face in the cloud, determination to remember it all life long.
Horses pictured on huge green waves of mountainside.
Three sharks in the bed of the bounty hunter's pick-up.
A crossroads near somewhere in a warming dawn.

I don't know if it's when I'm waking or asleep
that I meet her again, but I wait for those times.
Happiness of wandering, let it never be time's up.

NOSTALGIA

While I was dreaming a Palmyra of the north—
porticos and severe broad ramparts
shining through ice and pine, with tall stone stairs
down to the frozen seashore from rock walls
and the high rock bluffs they grew from,
and my love, new to my terrible city, on my arm,
her grey-green eye following wide where I pointed
to every titan miracle—I came to
that corner. How far, dream-walking, had I wandered
through long blocks of houses, how many miles,
forgetting I was in a sort of mortuary
or barrack, being watched by the sleepers
or the dead? And then: the corner. Why
did I wake there, at that crossway with its closed
and faintly glowing store, and a few faces,
a smile, a serious look, in the café window?
Its traffic light, exemplar of all duties
fulfilled in oblivion, timed the periods
to stop and go for no one, splashing its reds,
ambers, and greens on rain-wet asphalt. There,
I came to myself among an unknown people,
in a hidden life that always waits the same,
is waiting now, ready for me
to come across, I don't know where,
someplace in a city where I once lived.

Hospital

Your tender-heartedness for the poor
and for all puppets of the force that withers,
bloats, and eats us, was eminent among
the many messengers that brought your image
daily to my mind. I saw you, poor yourself
beyond my own desertion, your small hand
outstretched and palm downturning, drop
your offering, appalled, into the mirror
hand of the leper mother with no face left
in dust mountains. How far by then
hope and fear to be absolved
from our luck had driven you
away from home. Her three children
clung to her, hung in space from the dry, thin,
weathered torso, and she and they are yours,
you carry them. You kiss them when your glance
closes before its other double, the Pacific
evening, and you are in your dark
and partless time of no refusal. Nothing
can stop you in your living time from plunging
into desolate prison and hospital
where all together stretch to touch
your hem. But you don't see those hands. You see
backs deformed and turned and yourself ghostly,
wandering unobserved.

CASSANDRA

You'll lose the power to believe your dreams,
you said when you were leaving, and they'll decay
from heart-made worlds to fear of this one. I wouldn't
believe, Cassandra, but you came back last night
to my sleep and I had to admit again (in the rubble,
the few pieces of us remaining) the senility
of dream that you predicted, and how it would kiss
the old days—the young days—with its small shadow.
My dream of you was this: we were together,
you, me, and the ones we've loved more and married,
and you said: Let's all go to New York. I was shrinking,
hidden in a corner of the next room, naked,
plotting a dart into the shower, ashamed
of body, dirt, unreadiness. I calculated:
how could I come? Just thirty-six hours between
tonight's appointment and Monday's. And I hated
the coward who was powerless to throw
the scheduled world away, a crumpled bill.
My nakedness I felt no longer sex
and angelhood: a thin sense of earlier dreams
came back to me in the form of an invisible dust
darkening that miserable pageant with a scrim
of gold. God, I thought in sleep, are you looking down
and hating me because I promised once
to be different and collapsed into the usual
darting frightened eyes? And yet that dream
was Eden since you were here as firmly, tersely
as in the daylight of touch. Cassandra, come
and bring me back the other dreaming. Restore,
improve the old dream of opening you that was

tenderness you gripped. Sit by me on the floor
of the gymnasium again in the naked chatter
of boys and girls, our friends, and cut out streamers
and crepe paper stars for next week's dance, our heads
touching, hair marrying. Forgive me, ask God
to forgive me that my heaven, my desire,
is nothing but school days, and even that comes back
only in shreds of a dream I can't see anymore:
the glimpse of halted adolescence, of laws
and sentences always dodged, always suspended,
where you left me and I go on courting you.

Failure

To say these words may fail is late.
No one hears them, their nudity and costumes
of feathers and veils and filthy rags
were not the styles that anymore fascinate
interpreting or cataloguing gazes.
And when they were held secretly, withheld,
coddled in silence, they did not deliver us
a satisfactory world. Not even you alone
have they found and freed,
leaving me here to pay
with boredom of bare floor, displastic naevus, bending
spine, and narrowing vision, for my prayer:
that you find safety where the night in your smile,
that light of the good moment
longing for something more, is not
a slavery in a city-like
hell of clay huts and heaps of broken brick.
And you'd rebuke the words, if you could hear them,
rebuke their description of the world, the one
we have, and the only imagination they bring me now
is seeing that I don't know of any just
or adequate day
to give you, even show you, if I could ever
in this life that's ending once wake by your side.

CHILDISH WILLOW

I will let the tree stand
for many things they took away:
they cut you down, willow, my pavilion
of childhood, your leaves
were other birds and fish than those we know
in the streams and the air, another veil
of appearances around us, infant and naked
company, your height and spread another sky
that would admit the first and higher sky,
the blue one, through little gaps, as a guest.
They deprived me of you and locked me
screaming in my room until
your excision should be over,
and waited for time, which erases everything,
to calm me down and here I sit
decades later, maybe eons, I don't know,
like a smudged paper rubbed
to brittle thinness. The former marks on it
indeed are gone, almost, but the slightest stroke
would now tear through, so nothing
ever is written there. But surely it's evil
to stay a blank like this,
now that I'm grown and could destroy them,
evil to lie rubbed thin and yet untorn,
not to recut the faint scars,
and ooze, and howl.

The Call

I have a more ardent nature than all those who have seen visions
or seized power, rising from their windowless earthen basements
three stories deep in the river mud on the atrocious old north side
that people once called Indian Town. I went down to the plaza,
it was so hot in my little vault, to feel the air,
and how many mad red spiders, smaller and more distracted
than my pencil point, did I kill, sitting under a tree combing my hair?
You will hear inwardly, I remember them telling me, you will know.
I went out again later to listen by the fountain where the runaways squat.
Nothing definite has befallen me. I took my pencil and sketched
an idea: the word is something endless like heat or snow.
But a word needs its completion, a moth from the streetlight said,
and who knows what it is? Maybe it's like your wound for her
who is dead, and then they tell you she's too little for God to recall.

Memorial

I don't want a memorial of love
that someday another man or woman will see,
opening a book or wandering under a hill,
and say: "Of him, we learn his name, and she...
he left her blanker still—
whether it was through the error of restraint
or through how little art can do or will,
who knows? In any case this, so faint,
blank almost, is their memorial,
that we can only make what may please us of."
I don't want a memorial of love.

What We Had

I really did love you in a sense, colleagues,
friends and fellow citizens and passersby
of my day here, who stormed the smoking world,
struggling to plant your flags or at least be heard.
I looked at you with consistent and unfeigned
interest, delighted in the revelation
of your pointless variety. It was joy to know
myself a poet among so many who knew
it also, but kept it quiet — the one thing
you did keep quiet. So many males and females
of divers pretensions: fortified handmade heights
from which in rage and fear you each would look
downward at me and melt in love. And I
would melt too and would feel the sympathy
of living with you among the flowers and rocks,
and dream sometimes for long seconds on end
that all any of you wanted was blessèd life
for everyone, and me too. But she and I
clung to each other, comrades, and I understood
that you more truly were the storm, and though
the two of us are dead now, what we had
to do in life, in fact, was to survive you.

RETURN TO THE FOUNTAIN

Before these skies that are the eyes of the many
blind or dead somewhere. Before these stones
travelling at random slowly on the lot
with all their shadows: clots of blood, minstrels
wandering the juvenile earth. Before the songs
like spools of ribbon, white and blue, for wrapping
wrinkled bulks. Before the whirled slings of minutes,
I used to write to you concerning fountains.

How a fountain is a tree whose bark is idea:
transparency, and vague but strict direction—upward—
hold formless fluid in the perfect form of dancing.
From the shade of acacias, from a stone bench,
we saw the nudity and grizzled strength, and the nudity
and fleeting slenderness, of the old fountain, its pouring
beards and manes. Its tinkling of decay became
our pleasure. And I think you'll never leave me.

On a far-off plain, but clear and close as in
a muraled basin, bright under trembling water,
the horses wheel, their riders play with lances
that long ago broke off in purple throats,
and one breaks off from the pack and galloping
in a cool strong wind to a girl beneath an elm
he catches her up like silk. Where will they go?
Why are we sure, from this distance, she desires him?
The western sky with the sun is blue, the eastern
black, the gold comes pouring over the city

and corn fields, and reapers can be heard
singing, the master song. The little ill-kept fountain
we found in a back street, mouldering away:
what a great house it proved itself to be.

GIACOMETTI

No, yes, a tree,
a man, a water
fall will never
stop flowing earth
to sky, not
even if
they should be
come nothing. Some
times the perfect
sculpture of scending
matter is disturbed,
the live column
catacombed by winding
holes like those
that worms and bullets
live in
and leave. So air
and light mine
into and through the slender
fluid when over
rock it slips and
stretches out and twisting to
almost severed
emaciation is
made more
apparent in
the violated
state of bright
foam.

POET AND SISTER

Late at night I was reading the great poet
whose mind's a beautiful woman, my own sister,
the one who died young, by him brought back to me
in a dream not a dream but a poem, and now
(through a long life I never knew she had,
a life I thought they'd stolen from her) grown
to perfection of woman that was lost in me.

How, in the black, hard, imperial
Roman marks his language shares with mine,
did he revive the pain and softness of every animal,
fountains, children's grimy nudity
glimpsed through their rags, a sky of roses,
an earth, a thought of roses, golden dust
under the feet of bleeding bulls and cocks,
the cripples, the procession of wooden saints?

I read him too late to discover: the dawn came,
he said goodbye, and his mind (my sister,
his loving wife) said goodbye. Then let them know
that I am here and will continue being slaughter
and triumph of barbarians, high walls and burning
scattered stones, a blue sky and a soldier
who looks up, dead, in the black imperial
Roman traces his language shares with mine.

IN A PROSPEROUS COUNTRY

At Two Solemn Musicks

We sit in the wind gloating on our lump
of sorrow. Then we move along sidewalks, I mean through forests,
under trunks, walls, cranes, signs, branches and windows
singing, O susurration
of leaves, wires, groins, high iron, moon
on scaffolding. But over there—
I like it better over there than here where we are:
there they stomp around a trash fire
to insultingly stupid honkings that litter good silent air.
Sometimes they too are quiet and melancholy as we are here.
Sometimes one of them or a whole family will close the door
and commit suicide in simple despair.
But that is sometimes. Now, how thin the sorrowful
painted face of the petrified moon here has become
that over there is the bell of a trombone:
its high white note and black mellow note
hurt alike and as long as they are not dead
in last spasms they live.

The Ant

The splendour and simplicity
That sealed my childhood eye
Are dearer than the world now is,
And like the dews that lie
On grass tips to be drunk while down
Beneath them, ants pass by.

The ants pass to their morning work.
Do they sleep through the night
Like children, or work on and know
Nothing of dark and bright?
And if they never sleep, is work
Their sadness or delight?

Angelic was the child I was,
Who followed the black ant
With sight from heights he could not see
And let that supplicant
Wander as lost as lost he seemed
All morning, till I went.

How could a question not occur?
But I absorbed his pain,
If pain it was, or his pure joy,
And found him, the same one
Or one just like him, searching still
When morning came again.

Thou Poem

Thou poem of lost attention and half try,
do you fear more the inner world or outer?

I do not love the self less than the others,
my name is legion and my mouth one cry.

Thou poem of the unwell, of the dry well and doom,
and the snake's on your lip, in you the toad persists.

Did we come here just to read of what exists?
I champ at my winter bit to be in bloom.

But what's the difference between you, poem, and the flower?
Don't both break from the compost as long as it may be?

You are the one who knows what metaphor
and imposes it. Two dandelions are not similar to me.

Thou song of all-powerful individuality,
if only I could rest in you escaping me…

You would never again be troubled by the nudity
of the mother, or the Heart Fall's killing roar

as you slid toward it, catafalqued on the fluid
descents of a new old world, shrouded in greenwood.

Thou ignorant epic of half-knowing ever more,
thanks in thought's ruin for reminding me.

Philosophical Content

I know that words should shriek in pain and gleam
like a cat's fur, like beautiful black and white
starkly opposed—the night and light, the day and sea—

on the one supple sufficiency of her body.
I know that tears fall into the pit and rise
like the cries of a pink mouth: the beast's, the pet's

instinct of desperation, her confidence,
in the measure and delay, starvation's threat,
of the fragile food supply, in the poor human house.

Old Pet

Come, my body, leap up, while you still can,
onto my knees, into my lap. Come let me pet you,
comfort you and take comfort while there's time,
while you last. How calm you are: content, it seems,
with your infirmity, your age, in the almost changeless
youth of your soft hide, your pelt and shy quiet,
expressionless as you huddle and crouch for this leap
you can still make, though it's grown great, this petty
piece of your young and many springs.

Why did I never, body, cherish you enough?
Although I thought I was spending all my minted hours
on you, till I'd cry at the long waste of time, chained
by eyes and tongue, the ends of every extremity,
to your pleasure. Now I can't recall ever once
kissing you, lying locked in you, deep as I want.

You'll die, it won't be long, body, swiftly
in animal nobility—how you wear your decline unnoticing,
the way a poor man walks in his only shirt to work—
and then, without you, in what mud of my own
making will I linger, falling apart? Purr now
and fuse your old pleasure into crotch of my torso,
palm of my hand, vision of eyes and sag of diaphragm
inseparably: they're yours. Give me your indifference
that a once forest-wide range comes down
to couch and counter now, and this lap. Give me
your unrepentant having-known

a more-than-ant's-intimacy with the grass,
a more-than-god's-innocence in the hunt,
a greater-than-winged-agility in branches
and light. Leap up, body, while you still can,
let me finally hold you, feel you, close enough.

Swiftness no longer trusted,
you were my voice, flickering
lines and ideas in violet shade
and green sun: goldfinch wing-strokes
keeping impossible
fragments of flight—moments
of wing-folded hurtling
in the air—linked and aloft: the bird
would flurry its wings and close them,
careen along and imperceptibly
fall, then beat out again, rise,
hurtle again and fall, and so
always, along the bank, as sweet
as pencilled breves and macrons marking
the syllables down a line
of Vergil in an old
schoolbook, or the droop
of wires from pole to pole
beyond Mesopotamia on a long road
when corn is ripe and a cloud's
a golden bat or butterfly,
or a hawk stooping from the sunset, so
we stop our car, terrified
for the moment to pass, and it passes,
fireflies come out and climb
through trails of spice
and now the world-colour is
of cooling sea,
of still rhythms and space.

In a Thunder Shower

Cardinal singing in the rain, what was your name
before there were these prelates in scarlet capes
we call you after? Who were you in old plain style,

before our age and this decadent decoration
of rule we've made our shame, but accept, and in you,
in the singing hierophany you bring into

the imperial word you're stuck with, even revel in?
Your voice starts up again and is straightway crushed
by a crossing overhead of vagrant thunder. You stop,

you wait for a pause, appear to believe all's clear,
and sing. And there's your secret—always starting again,
speaking, whatever you're called, red crest and wing.

It's hard to improve on the poetry of a bus,
a city bus—whether full of passengers,
friends and strangers, or with no one but the driver,
or empty, dead in the water of lot or barn:

a box with wheels and windows. Empty form
waiting for content. And yet, how form alone
makes a clear statement, although just what it says
is hard to say. Then the driver pulls it out,

it streaks through storm, now flashing Not In Service
from its radiant forehead, polluted and obscured
by splattered mud, till it can reach its station

and help to ease the overflow of us
waiting in anger. Then we all barge in
and improbably improve the poetry of the bus.

KURT MAZUR'S EARS

They're immense and baroque, not in the least
romantic, Kurt: two relief maps of Argentina
hung there, each lobe a land of fire
with farther north the pampas and the city
of mirrors, mazes, folds, the bandoneón's
savage sadness. But what I want to ask is,
how just by stirring an invisible cup of tea
with tiny ovoid strokes before
your fourth shirt button, then throwing in
six, seven, eight, ten lumps of non-existent sugar
with elegant bird-dartings
of a high held right clutch of fingers,
do you cock Adriatic sun up
this black fish shaped and smelling eastern
American night? Maybe the hundred harmless
soldiers beneath you, each with a self-willed
anarchic choice of antiquated weapon,
drilled a long life to earn mere rising, falling
into the pits of those ears. Maybe their size
can hear (but why, then, couldn't LBJ's?)
Mendelssohn away in Leipzig, 1833,
listening for Posilipo and the Italian sea.

Is that the full moon and its dark bruise-like markings,
or the shadow of a man in a slouch hat with crumpled brim
looking in at our blackness through a round window
beyond which lies a flat buckwheat-flour light?
There's really no question: simply, the one it is
"looks like," "reminds me of" the one it's not.
It's as though some great hunter who was also a great singer
sang: "I lay in wait all of a night and a day and a night
for the young deer to move, trying not to fall into a dream
of her sweet fat. Then I could wait no longer:
was she a demon, never blinking, stiller than a rock?
I notched my arrow and crept up, waiting for her to bound
beyond me, tasting the disappointment to come
if she should sniff me too soon. But she
never stirred and I came close enough to grab her heart
in my fist. She was just shadow among the tree trunks
and all my strength against sleep had been for nothing.
I was asleep and dreaming from the start. I the hunter
was a dream my hunger had, a dead stock standing in the forest
a night and a day and a night." And his song was deeply loved,
the most intoxicating song, but now there's no one left
who knows it because his whole race, all twenty of the people,
died the end of that summer in the drought.

The Jar

We found a jar there. Not a vase, not a piece of the potter's art
but glass, from a store shelf, with a threaded mouth,
the lid and label long gone, all residue of the product blotted away:
bright crystal. I had to tell you this because the word jar
dwells in between comprehending both. It reminded us of songs we know,
the "broken water jar," the "jar in Tennessee," the "drinkin' liquor
from an old fruit jar." But the desolating place: white weeds,
white ground baked into sharp lumps and ridges,
a dead sapling, bushes crisp with thirst, rattling in a breeze.
No moisture in the jar. No way to tell if it had been thrown away
or washed and kept as a vessel. We succeeded for a while in seeing
the curves and sun-glints of its strange perfect hollow with affection.
We felt shaken, imprisoned, as though the low whine of the acres of flies,
as though the silence, were aftermath of a deafening shout. We longed
for wet darkness, even if it brought that doom-laden bird, the nightjar.

IN A PROSPEROUS COUNTRY

In a prosperous country I without wealth or power
am final proof of the nonsense of meaningful song
to the true poor. They did not freely choose a course
any fool would know leads to poverty. Simply, bombs fell
on their Sarajevo or Eritrea of dreams. They were hoeing,
or smoking in a café and mentally outlining an article,
when shells thumped and sniper rounds ping'd from foliage
on neighbouring hills they'd never given much thought to:
beloved and ignored background of a world. Simply,
drought came. The sun conspired with the government
or with the rebels to cut off all passage to the sea.
Nothing but hunger for a hundred miles in all directions
and the pity of foreign journalists awaiting
their airlift out. The true poor know now with certainty
they would not be so stupid as to scorn wealth and power,
if luck ever let them live again in a prosperous country.

THE GIRLS

His skin is loved by morning. He sits in it almost naked
and the girls think his sweat—mild sweat of the sun,
not acid of war or labour—is enough to clothe him.
Yesterday he got up at dawn, fought with his sex and voice
all day, and at the end it seemed necessary, before sleep,
to savour some darkness. Outside his house: towering
lilac beyond a wooden wall, the wide warm lake of scent,
purple of the flower bunches in streetlight, brick walls
with brightly painted doors, and bags and cans of garbage
waiting for morning. Night long he absorbed the stillness,
thinking what an antiquated image is a man alone.
Shouts came from lighted crossings somewhere. When day rose,
he looked the same as ever, a powerful and soft
form of impatience. Mask of rapacity and headache.

The Tidal Wave

One day I'll wake and see the tidal wave above my city
fulgurating at its dripping diamond crest in the sun
like another, a nearer, sun, and its sheer wall
under its beautiful crown of spume will be
a vertical plain wider than any on earth, a bare steppe
but of flesh, flesh of planed and planished liquid
teak and jet and jade.
How tall will it be—three miles, a hundred miles? How far
or imminent? Will there be seconds or years
before it falls on us? I only know it won't matter anymore
that I was sick in mind. Under the shadow or in the light
of the wave I remembered childhood,
when I dewinged a moth, inspected
the writhing tube and then forgot, went elsewhere.
And manhood, when the memory came back one day
twenty years later and so I couldn't reach the moth
to give the gift of murder, impose release
on its horror as the pure ignorance
of my imagination created it
and felt it. This I thought of every day and hour
to the exclusion of battling like everyone
with everyone for the bread reserved
to others. I slipped into alley mouths
and doorways among empty buildings and occupied
myself all day with saying my nightly prayers, O God
please take away the carcinoma, aphasia, ataxia,
the monomania, hysteria, dementia from her
and him, the age from them, aren't they old
enough already, why should they have to get
still older, till the list of them

became so long that many died
as I forgot them, as my day
became not long enough to run through the vast roll
and pronounce it all. I lost
who they were in the bourdon of their names
rumbling in me, shaking the frame
till I thought my ears were bleeding and I clawed
my skull—but nothing was happening there, in fact I,
the face that faced it, looked roseate, glimpsed
in dark windows, and cheerful. A conscious eminence
absorbed in guilt and supplication, scraggy psalms,
while the citizens ran on and soon forgot
the ones at the gate fallen
with broken leg and twisted bowels and waiting and hoping
to be shot. But when the wave appears
above the city, all this will proceed as usual,
it's what we know, and the absolute equality
of what I do and what they do, my strength and theirs,
will appear in the water's black and crystal glow.

The one who watches while the others sleep
does not see. It is hoped, it is to be hoped
there is nothing to see. The camp has quieted
behind him and all is peace there—let it be—
at his back, where he longs to turn his face
and see the walls of pitched cloth that hide
his comrades, sleeping. But lights go down, and out,
and if he turned there would be nothing, black,
with just the bulks of looming tents aglow
with just the memory of last evening's light.
Likewise, nothing to see in the outward
dark before his face, where there is nothing,
it is to be hoped—only a darkness
of useless vigilance, unless it is a darkness
of hostile conniving lights not lit out there,
surrounding treachery, faces smeared with ash
to blend in with the night and lying low.
And what if morning ever comes, when things
are just as always, it's obvious to all?
Won't he have to find some commander and report
everything he observed? Out and beyond
the perimeter, he notes nothing that may not be
a moth fluttering or a shooting star
behind thick cloud. Within the camp, though,
constant stirrings. Sudden snorts as if breath
cut off by some torturer was suddenly permitted,
the hands unclenched from the throat at the last
second before death. And longer, steady snores,
woodmen in snowy forests. Whimpers of mothers'
and pet dogs' names, uncertain breezes moist

with tears and snot fluttering the tent flaps,
men curled up knees to nose and heels to hips
like ringed camps and feeling only
the anus's openness and the back a target,
or stretched out straight, cupping and tangling fingers
in hair and cooing to the genitals as if
to a girlfriend. Fart, belch, and vomit,
urine, dirt and sperm falling in latrines,
shuffle of feet on stones, books, letters, pictures
felt for under brittle pillows and the dreams
of bleeding inwardly, of growing a third arm,
of removing the penis like a banana from its skin
and passing it around the campfire, vaguely anxious
the others won't pass it back. But
the commanders, wouldn't they tell him:
What good's this report? You saw nothing
you were supposed to see. You wasted your time
listening to us, but we knew where we were
and what was going on here. And you saw only
the obvious and trivial and drew the worst conclusions.
Or drew no conclusions, it's simply that the obvious
always looks filthy: any obstruction you can't pass
or at least see through takes the form to you
of a rotting cellar wall aswarm with worms.
Besides, none of this ever happened. You
made it up to humiliate us, you are a foreign
agent, which is why no hint of the enemy's
numbers, movements, or power ever appears
anywhere in your lying reports. You fell asleep
at your sacred post and this report records
your evil dreams, a spontaneous creation you love
and so a deeper shame to you than if
you had rationally constructed out of sheer depravity

this libel on your comrades. And who
appointed you at all? You are not the sentinel.
The sentinel has already given his intelligence,
which we are analyzing. You are the lonely watcher,
the one who won't sleep until it's time to work,
the one who wants a salary and a title
for insomnia. If we have nightmares,
it's that we hear your footsteps under our window,
wake up, look out along the street: no one.
That's what they'll say. And yet the report
will have to be filed, the storm endured. But not till dawn.
It is almost possible, it would almost be possible
to enjoy this fogged-in darkness, this dewfall and
rustling silence, the accustomed expectation
of receiving the first shot if indeed the enemy
has chosen tonight, except that one can't relax,
each detail must be noted or the report
will be a lie. In fact through no fault of his own
the sentinel will miss something, and the report
he contemplates, or the refusal to report
he also contemplates, will be a traitorous lie.
To light a match might well draw fire. He strikes,
it doesn't catch. But no, it sputters, waits,
then flares. He moves it to his lips, and peace.

PLACE

I woke up in a place familiar and alien,
like someone forgotten, someone I had loved,
even coupled with, years ago, or last night
in a dream that won't come back. And if I lacked
even these traces? I turned to a stone of fear.
What if I'd never met my love and passed her
now on this sidewalk—would I have the power
to know her, or have I fallen too far away
from what the boy could see? I looked around me:
no one. The face of the old monument was grey
with August heat. In the shut-up jeweler's window,
just the bottom of an empty ring box. But behind
the dimly known, derelict street there opened
others I'd never seen: a circular boulevard
with towering stores and mills in pyramids
and cylinders of ruby brick, and terraces
of houses carved out of single stones, glowing
on a steep green-tressed slope. Then I remembered
the molecular diagrams she used to send to me
in her letters: I'd look and see her eyes, where each
thing that exists tumbled yet held all space
like a ring in a box. And O, I thought, if only
I could go back and write her, why did you go
and what are you doing there, love, my only place.

Sad streets that even these weeks of softening rain
from flat, frayed, over-laundered, wearing skies
cannot make sadder. Some of them wander south
out of the business district, pick up small mills
and boarded buildings of antique cream brick
with horizontal iron poles above the doors,
poles for long-gone signs to swing on, stretching
across the crumbled sidewalks. Some of the streets
are edgeless lava flows of blacktop that pass
and isolate rows of houses with human heads
stacked in the windows looking out at the nothing to look at—
moon signals of the bodies' lament, nowhere to be,
have to be here—and cars retained in drives to keep alive
a dream of crossing over. This is my home.
But I am also from an invisible world
where we refused to kill and eat our god,
erasing him thus, and disdain to worship now
even irony. Each of us is supremely disabused,
so all are equal, proud and sick of being
sure of the shifting story on the helpless screen.
How there could I be great? So I came back
here, where I walk now—or, to be honest, drive—
and glimpsing lives and rusted lawns and houses,
cells of lives, can say the glance of God
holds each, no doubt unique and valuable,
and the quiet flatness of my creditless voice,
flanked by some body shops and bowling alleys,
mounts the ridge between my love's town and mine.

Secure in the success of the ruse that she was sunk, the *Titanic*
circles in the seas. The crew and passengers, who agreed to the great
experiment, love to watch movies of their replicant corpses bobbing
in frigid water, and bold explorers diving in the duplicate false wreck.
Human mythology, the waste of life to plumb the inconsequential bizarre,
disaster-fascination and the entertainment bonanzas it discloses —
now all this strikes them as remotely disturbing, faintly amusing,
tolerable. Their numbers swelled by those from the *Marie Celeste*
and the first Jamestown settlement and the abandoned cities
of the Maya classic period, they have formed a superior society,
based on the ideas of their high council members, Amelia Earhart,
John Kennedy, Ambrose Bierce, B. Traven, Arthur Cravan, and Elvis Presley.
They have storybook marriages and free love, eminence and equality,
a war on poverty and universal wealth, a dream and no need
to dream. The endless ship powers forward into the night of the sea,
the chaotic exact self-reproduction of the mass of waters,
cleaving a furrow from earth's core to the Van Allen Belt,
wrapping its wake around the moon. The age of the great liners
and their ports and piers has passed but it doesn't matter, or rather
the pre-jazz dance orchestra plays on and on in the salon
with an insouciance that infinitely surpassed it doesn't matter,
and on viewscreens with cardboard knobs, like those in the old
Flash Gordon serials, the passengers watch all that has occurred
in this world since that prophetic date: my birthday, 1912.
They know far more about our lives than we do, just as we do
when we spend the night watching TV documentaries about the years
we spent at university (who knew we were shaping history?) —
the night, when we ought to, we have to, be working but we're not:
just as we used to behave at university, passing all nights
and their necessities in diversions of the past. What good is it,

the Titanians debate and sing in their *eisteddfodau*, for us to be
(at least they're asking the question) so successfully hidden
that no one's angry and terrified at the conspiracy of our spiriting away?
Why does the world just accept that we're dead? And they glance
evilly at Hitler taking his constitutional around the deck,
tripping occasionally on the wires that connect him
to his brain in the tank in his stateroom; they mutter resentfully
at the Roswell alien emerging from the barbershop with his dome
fresh-shaven. The four stacks belch black, the stoker shovels coal,
the screw turns, the captain turns the wheel, some passengers recall
Whitman, Kafka, Henry James, and Boethius, while the *Titanic*
moves of its own accord, and all aboard, like the angels of God,
labour and think without purpose or effect, granted an office,
some compensation for the fact that fate and death are unreal.

Vermin; or, Weariness

Soon as the garden's planted, soon
as sugar's in the cupboard, you hear stiff wings
that broadcast on the air like mummy skin.

At night twelve electronic eyes
catch the most microscopic light and bore
poor darkness to the dollar in your pocket.

How the pelts gleam—violet, ecru, and umber—
and feathers nod cloud-wise, careless
that they will one day be hats or parts

of the refuse they revel in. Thwack,
thwack thwack, you are belabouring
their plushy ribs with a broom handle

where they have vice-presidentially overturned
the garbage can and spread the repast,
brown chicken bones, black plastic scraps.

Strategically, good generals, from cracks
behind you now come tinier blinder swarmers
into the room, the home front you've abandoned.

Here some of them managerially
are carrying home corpses of squashed others.
Here come the little hardened tar-hued

computer experts to the weekend blood tavern
to enjoy when they're let off work. Here come
the big and little thieves—the chief

executive officers (seven times seventy
billion strong) of the rooftree, on their way
to eat away the rooftree,

walking over the sticky mounds you slew
with your poetic insecticidal clouds.
Here descend the claws that cannot learn

from the death of their spouse of yesterday,
here shut the mandibles that cannot remember
the smashed abdomen of an hour ago,

here scrabble the claws ignorant
of the starvation of last year that flowed
from eating every last fish. Here

come the buzz, the mating screech,
the public relational suck and chomp,
the advertised locust roar in the corn,

the commissioned report on the necessity
of digging up the final root,
the final nut from the old

breast-like earth hanging from your chest
like an empty purse. Quit scraping
the fleas from your once shapely shins,

put down your gun and cry. There go
ten gallons of their untended droppings
and cadavers into the five-gallon crypt

of your X-blue lake. There go
six fine fat frisky fellows
with twelve tulip bulbs in their teeth.

IDEAL SONG OF THE COMMUNISTS

We are old, so old it hurts. After our long struggle
to reach the garden, we slept awhile in a straw chair,
then woke and wrote the poem of our white hats lying beside us,
light sprinkled all around by the olive trees, cicadas
hissing in a high register we can still hear, a male sparrow
chasing his female in thick vines. Beneath it all we lay,
a memory of some young and angry men and women
who disdained to be heroes. The symbols they used to paint
by night on city walls—red stars and sickle moons—
had been a better sky that would rise one day, a zone of free
and brilliant bodies above the city's black regiment.
It was an error, that dream: another slavery entered
through the eye of freedom. But they'd been beautiful,
naked in their naked error. So we took a new sheet and wrote
the poem of how they dazed us once, and it was right.
As we wrote that day, in the poor rocky harbour foreign ships
were unloading electronics, and this cottage shook
with trucks on the former sheep track. Glass towers go up:
nothing will ever happen here again, and we're at the climax
of our poem and our wakeful moment, about to slip back into
another dream in the sun, a bad dream, about you. If you
ever find what we've written, you'll be sad for the full moment
it takes to read these pages, on which the old ones once
despaired, joining the two ends of their life in a garden.

Cleanliness

Dead flies on the windowsills, the corpses now
of more than one summer, weightless but unstirred,
on the third story at the top of the stairs.

Impossible for her to climb them now.
Too much tiredness. But she will still
go there again some day, she promises.

Will rest the bucket and sponge on every step
and breathe, waiting for the water to stop
sloshing in the pail and her heart to stop beating.

Even if every step's an hour, a threat of death,
the attic will be clean again. We watch.
We notice the streaked tableware, the dust,

chipped things, and flecks of old food lying here,
on this first floor, its clearly dirty windows
beyond the ladder of her eyes, while in her words,

in her thought, only the lament goes on
for the space above, that it's filling up with webs,
that its contents, our pasts, are waiting to be given

or thrown away. And how much we'd give now
for the oppressive cleanliness that once
reached every day, angrily, into the least

and darkest corners of our childhood
to show us its vigour again, that fearful
enemy we won our best days in opposing.

Zoo Keeper

We watched the old zoo keeper,
the tigers sleeping,
haul them in their supper.
We saw him slipping

as he lugged the meat, heavy
and red, in the cage
through urine and water…a gravy
of various sewage

he later mopped up, his joints
snapping: we could hear.
Then he's done and a child points:
the tigers stir,

roused by the closing door's click.
He was gone, forgotten,
as we watched them shamble to lick
their slumped, blood-sodden

food. And I was the keeper
of my own breast.
Did my fierceness go any deeper
than my self-served feast?

Ease, ease, ease
is all I love,
to salve, satisfy, erase
what makes me move.

Arrogance

They easily recognized the reprehensible arrogance
of the poet vilifying "a whole population
that goes about its business and doesn't know
it is no longer human." They on the other hand
valued common things: a day at work at a screen or a window,
noon in sunny streets, bright signs, the office girls
showing their legs as they ate sitting on concrete banks
in the plaza by city hall. They acknowledged that to walk
at such times past the form lying against a wall,
wrapped with thick blankets despite torturing humidity,
shamed them and assured them they were alive. Too vague
a claim, they admitted, doubling back honestly on themselves,
vague as a billboard: I am alive. So trying to be clear
and fair, they felt like passengers who believe
when they are told it won't be so bad up ahead
where the crowded train is taking them,
it will be worth the long journey herded
offensively close with many others, developing for a few
who happen to be jammed nearby a necessary,
compensatory love. It won't be so bad. It will even
be better. After all, each stage of the journey
so far has been tolerable: maybe
the seeming steady decay in conditions is in truth
only ageing, a tendency to discomfort
and querulousness, one of the common things,
decline of their capacity to endure.

The Shore

A woman walked by the empty sea
and the only stars there: the lame moulds
of her footprints, and longed-for
crowds that used to crowd
that frigid beach, those waters only motion
keeps from becoming ice: tritons,
and cod swarms on a black wave
smothering in their congress
of mortised and tenoned bodies, and graeae
lassoing the grampus and narwhal,
mermen mating with and sating
mealy tunny. And she thought:
without that abolished company, here
is eternity—silver scallops
of sand in oblique light at cold
golden misty sunups, and a stunned
mind filled with nervous water.

The Moment

It is the moment when something must be done
and in this it is like every other moment
and one is ignoring it
and in this it is like every other moment
and it has disappeared without disaster, benefit, or trace
and in this it is like every other moment.
And one doesn't know if the tingling in the legs is a mortal disease
just making its first showing, or fear.
It is the moment when something must be done
but the telephone rings in a fire station down by the distant lake
and a blimp passes above a man training dogs in a narrow back yard
and a screen door slams adding the final drop that makes nervousness
overbrim miles away and run down the hot black street.
Also a desultory guitar gets sick for the moment and drags
the fingers of the picker into a definite illness
and also wilted daisies are brought home from a store because they
                                                      were cheap
and are stuck in some water but nothing will revive them
but there they are, beautiful nonetheless and dropping gold
and purple petals all over a yellowing
paperback copy of And Then There Were None,
but the culprit slinks away drenched in a sudden brilliant storm
that has arisen to prevent the detective from reading to the end.
The moment has come when one must go to bed
and quench the ever-intensifying restlessness in darkness.
Otherwise it will catch fire and be day again,
there will be no more darkness, no more rest,
and in this it will be like every other moment.

Sound of Hungry Animals

There was a sound of hungry animals at night
or animals in the pain of their coitus
or the self-hatred of their inseparable pack
grieving, and beneath my conscious prayer
in the relief of the cool and humid darkness
the one spirit spoke betraying my desire
for some good of which I could never be aware.

BETTER DAYS

POEM OF COURTLY LOVE

I want to hate what is believed: that darkness
is first and silence best, that the good part
of the word is wind, and the adequate part
an image, that the chance part is the beginning
and the necessary part the end. I want
to sit with you, unable to understand
the book that holds all human story to be
an allegory of our dying
proposals of rebirth. I want this book
we were reading to slip from your lap
as you tremble, seeking courage to surrender,
so the interpretations woven insidiously into plot lines
lie face down in dust, and the story
that starts with your breast
opens in our air—nipples, eyes, tongues
and the words to come
happy in the pause
that is their natural home.

THE LIGHT

In your house
on the upper floor
one light is on
in a window open
like a mouth
saying "Oh,"
and it looks, it sounds
just like your breath.
No other light there
speaks to the night,
and below I see
the door in shadow
and its blacker mark,
the keyhole. If I
went up and forced it
and felt it give,
would I find you
somewhere, breathing,
maybe behind
that one bright window—
laid on a bed or
crouched in a closet
or pressed brow first
into the angle
of two white walls?
Or no one there?
No one, for you
had turned into
your house: I was
in you, so never

64

again could meet you
face to face, never
once more trace
the halls and,
reaching the only
room still lit
with its small bed
and folded-down sheet,
see you there and
see if you are
alive or dead.

The Red Car

Little red car in which I saw them drive away,
boy and girl with their curious striped cat in his cage,
with my map of the way to Michigan, ancient map
that shows Big Beaver Road and Bloomfield Hills
already lost in the wilds of Detroit, no bloom,
no field, no beaver, be the car I dreamed.
Be the little red MG I want for my wife.
You're only a rented pocket sedan, but be
that sportscar of a dire adventure that never fails.
This is the best of life, this instant, these years
of loving them on the edge of a black cliff
where their falling would turn the green earth to an ash,
to a mummy's lips, while it went on twinkling,
brushing my breast with its orange hair as if nothing
had changed. And what would have changed? Many
have died in the space of these lines. But little red car,
carry them safe and I will carry you safe.
I'll love you forever, as we say, my friend,
knowing perfectly
that memory and body disappear,
identifying ourselves with the long drive to reappearance.

PLEASURE CRUISER

The tiny windvanes whirl their props,
veer and adjust: black arrows, graceful
in the blue as military jets,
atop the masts of pleasure cruisers returning
to the inner harbour: *Comus, Ailsa, Luna Belle,*
passing down the slip of greasy foam and feathers.
Our backs, love, against the rusted iron
railing of that broken jetty, our feet against
steel mushrooms: mooring spools, now never used.
And on the opposite shore, the container port,
the forklifts busy among orange, white, and ochre
oblongs at Warehouse 52. The captain
of the *Comus,* no allegorist of chastity,
salutes us without words. And what to say
to the joys of his retirement? — his overloaded
duffel of bare abdomen tanned sandy brown,
and his wife, unloosed, buttocks in slow panic
escaping the black bikini as she squats,
blindly presenting towards us, to lift the ropes
and bicker with him on the wind. To banal
insouciance of the pleasure-eating body as it passes
our hope and disgust, say what, from these shores
of black work, where we sit and watch
it sun, it bob on the rhythm of black work?

Two Crickets

Cool darkness and no peace. In the room's black,
the ceiling swarms with smears of light cast out
from open eyes. Images never quite images,
parts of bodies yet to coalesce
in an always future hell. Outside, one cricket
singing with long still pauses—August is over.
And for the moment no one harries him
or pecks him up, he doesn't despise his own invention,
doesn't worry the song of longing he repeats
is ignorant, failing to know and bring all things
the wise and passionate will ever say of love
to his lady. Listen and you seem to be in his peace
under the leaves of an impatiens flower.
There's dew all over your body and a slight stir
fans it to further cold but you don't shiver. Who knows?
August is over, for the moment no one harries
or eats us, we sing stupidly free of doubt.

FLOWER IN THE CRANNIED WALL

Flower in the crannied wall,
wall ever wearing away, flower ever repairing,
wall ever dragged toward the condition of a sieve,
more space than stone, a finest filter, a scallop of lace
to embrace and manifest an unseen breast,
flower ever bound to find the condition of being a flower.
O simple clover I seem to be him grasping you,
your root, your naked legs and waist
dragged from your covering, where you grew,
from your home that you loved and despised, crying.
Forgive me if I seem to say I know
when I do not know and dying
I hold you ignorant
and wondering aloud. Let God close space
and give the day again when I first saw you
leaning back against the wall
and heard in the curve of your throat exposed
the leaf and purl of human flesh.

Final Flower

Somewhere right now you may rest
assured an old old hand
is putting on a grave the final flower
that will be put there. Too weak
to return, a rag of memory now:
the hand in the corner of its room,
nameless as a piece of cloth,
when a knocking at her locked door
begins and will continue
to the knocking on a sealed lid
and her grave, unremembered from
its first moment. But to return.
Grass will now grow over the flat stone
level with the earth that the hand
used to keep visible, restraining
the healing exuberance of nature
in case a chance comer here should want
to read. It is not known
that anyone ever read the stone
but it's possible, given how many
bicyclists, joggers, walkers, hobby
historians, drunks, and crazy shouters
wander here, idly eyeing
the dates, inscriptions, urns, and palms.
Even the most erased old limestone
at the foot of the most secluded slope
may be stumbled and pissed on
once a summer. From this stone,
when the flame of this last carnation
has gone, all distinction goes

forever, the blades of the rotary mower
alone will visit, passing over
amid the jet, light plane,
and helicopter noise. And so
I put this flower of ignorance
that cannot wilt on the hand and the stone,
and leave to wild conjecture
what it means, the ragged pattern
of the graves in rough ranks and files,
as if someone has stored and ordered,
but not too carefully, lumber.

DIOTIMA

When time, Susette, or time's cessation brings you again to
your Friedrich who once solaced you with his dark voice,
what groves along rivers will spring up again at your eyes,
your breasts, your fingers. A cry of encounter marries you.

You'll say your own dream then, not with lips he moved for you
when your mouth was in an earlier earth. And it will proclaim
justice of God. And a stag undying will drag the arrow in
its side through two joined heartlands, in memory of the hunter.

The gods decay to paler colours, more delicate forms,
monstrous. I use another language, crave another country,
but no one can wish you exile, much less a darkness of loins,

of senses. Watching as you wait in space spread out,
Apollo on a high promontory poses and is frozen,
an angering stone. Then, veils of rain come wrap your body.

MASTECTOMY

Fortunate one, you were chosen victim of
the worst injustice: life hates life. Your breasts
took suddenly that hue called pit,
the opposite colour of human flesh.
Your life was forcing on you freedom
from your life: and yet
it was for freedom that fire
became man, said the sad sage
with his never consummated burning.
Looking at you, I was given understanding
that my prayers for you were for another,
for a kind injustice, for myself: Give me,
the prayers were saying, always
a way to work, meaning: Part the crowd.
Part me the crowd in the terminal ward,
in the academy part it, make way for me
and at the trough give me my part,
the part that is the whole, make me
the pillar of fire, the column of water
that walks the land
undrunk, crystalline and revolving, free.
Make me
the one who has the world in hand
as the hourglass has the disease of sand.
Make her, make us, but make me
the container that cannot exist,
the vessel to hold all things shapely and forever
let me walk here and see.

THE SUN HE SAID

The sun he said would reappear
when it desired and shred the clouds
but I knew it had no such power,
that they might stay and strangle it
forever—only, they depart
of their own motion, never knowing
or willing where they go. They tear
and part, forget themselves, like men
forget their minds, like he himself
forgot himself when he declared
the sun would rip those curtains when
it pleased. He lay within, in beds
of overcast and wandering thought,
nervous and motionless, too wide
to fit in any name we give
emotions, say "despair." And then
as usual the clouds did open,
maybe they changed to dust and fell
or else a blue hand pulled them back
to show a blue breast, a blue womb
that stood above as though descending
to his intelligence and lips.

THE SOURCE

What would silence be? The song
of a tempered shining, almost too small
to hear—the song itself of the sun,
hushed as it is by distance, and so, hidden
in the ear's ignorance, but in good time
for no reason it comes to notice and then
plays beautiful by day, more beautiful by night,
and more, more beautiful by day?
Would it be like the furnace
noise out there, next to the cruel star,
where any listener who came near
would burn to a clinker, the sound that here,
beneath our air, where the listeners are,
becomes a song as soft as nothingness—
the central power I claim beginning
outside me, far, and dwindling its fire
into my core?

BEWILDERMENT

I love the bewilderment of God
when looking at you he wonders:
It was for her I created all the rest,

women, and men, and the animals,
and everything that, to underlie them,
had to exist — crystals, elements, forces —

and all that had to wait, showing the way
ahead and above: gods and demons,
prophets, gnostics, the All and Nothing,

the darkness before I am and which I built
as a bed. But was everything for her?
I wonder, because when I saw her

and in that first excitement invented wheat,
and reaped, threshed, milled, mixed, kneaded,
and baked, and tested the bread with my mouth

and my nose, each loaf, so that somewhere
in the succession from my oven and hand
she would occur, I had to devour every one.

They were all equal, perfect
copies of her, each different, differently
to be consumed. And I

determined to go on forever,
both before her lifetime and forever after,
producing her. But what's gone wrong?

Why won't they give her what she needs,
or give themselves what they all need,
when it's lying there in the world

where I put it, at her feet: just let
her be. Quit crimping, marching her,
demanding obedience. Let her follow

that law I read for the first time
when I thought her, when I heard her
reasoning freely by the rule she is.

But no: she's there in the middle
of their cities and ages, and all around her
are others all wrong. Whenever

he sees you this way incomparable on earth
then I love you, suddenly know you, call you
bewilderment of God come here.

DANDELION

Through the infinite limits of the night in ruins
the mumbler goes with his sounds but they're all one:
voices cut in pieces, pain that oozes
from the dead scars along this flat terrain
that channel dust past gardens and cottages.
Women come out and sniff him suspiciously:
the same old obsessive hatred of their sex,
flattering but lethal. And me too: I smell
his loneliness. How right to shake my head
and break the spell. I'm wondering again
why dandelions burn so terribly yet cool
on the ragged slope with its wild apple tree.
I'm five years old, absorbed, and soon will hate
the march each dawn I see to the plant gate.
But now to be back is right, my wife with me,
at naked five years old, the trackless field,
the dandelion fire and the wild apple shade.

THE FIRST, SECOND, THIRD, AND FOURTH

September came while we were on the road.
In a beautiful foreign city
we saw it erase
humid evenings, dawns sprinkled
with shadows, droplets, sparrows, and dust,
and hot blue noons of days devoid of rain.
On the night of the first, as if
a too human September had memorized
and marked the calendar, it used its old
gray cloud cloth with the tatters
and rents of light, and its elbow grease of wind,
to wipe the peeling paint on outdoor walls
and the posters for finished August festivals
of film, and dance, and poetry
clean of summer, and leave them more brilliant
with glistening wet. Cold air compensating
for muscular heat trapped in buttoned cloth,
the businessmen no longer sweated,
clodding up steep sidewalks, their bald spots on a level
with painted toes at the ends of long bare legs
of the eaters
of sweet rolls on elevated terraces.
On the second and third, girls on their way
to theatres, offices and libraries
still bared
navels
and thighs,
but the points of their high breasts
indicated unfailingly and only
a hard cold December at the end

of the evening. So on the fourth they gave up:
no more trying to turn autumn back
by walking past sex shops and Tibetan import stores
in meridional bareness. Better, even good,
to find the most flattering dark colours and thick fabrics
of the season coming. And when we ourselves
called the new September light
studious
and melancholy, we didn't mean
it studied or it mourned. It was only light,
and those girls with their fecund anti-awareness
of any regret would find
agreement in us. In fact, we were ahead of them,
it was they who scarcely aware had tried
for three long days to hold
on to that summer. The businessmen
were our better symbol for the moment,
though later we discarded
their memory: they sensed at once
it was cooler suddenly, easier
and more necessary to move.

THE SEER

The man was white, grey and pale brown,
the colourless colours of a used-up earth
where water has sunk down,
sunk down so low and risen
so far above the grey-white pale-brown heaven
and shrunk so far within itself
that it will not come back. What can moisten
a shrivelled water, or can a clod of ash
regain colours from the identical howl
of a white powder sun?

Not in me, he said,
ever again, but in the street
with engine and worker petals, not papery,
more fragile than that, there will be colour.
My eye will reach colour, all colours, every one
together, which no one will see in me
ever again.

I turned to the sky then
and it was all one blue, the colour of seeing,
and yet was as many blues, as subtle,
as tones of stubble in the most sunken cheek.

Her Work

I love to see you draw the hammer back.
It pauses there up in the air, a bird behind your ear
hovering to survey a vast country for one spot,
and it shines silver as light undercuts and buoys it
and my face shines too, reflecting its weighty
and polished determination pocked
with little flaws—now I feel them in my skin:
scars, dints of earlier strikes, or openings
for senses that want to be much deeper than they are
but still see only what's before them. The claw
scrolls out, is wind made stainless steel,
a breeze of someone's being about to run so freely
the mere intention lifts and curves his hair
into an ancient image of future power.
The wooden handle stabs the steel and the head
clutches the wood and your hand at the apogee
moves just a little without moving at all,
like upper reaches of a still tree, but the angles
at wrist and elbow, the distortion of the shoulder
are there now to vanish, stand in a forest
of vanishings: you bring the hammer down.

To the Still Unborn

You don't know me but I was once watching films and films
of yet another man-caused horror germinating in the depths.
I was sitting alone with a television's loud images of fear,
repetitious and badly made. I was wondering why
I couldn't turn them off. Always an outpost, a small
and stupid crew in some corner of sea floor, void, or desert,
was being assaulted by a beast that enters the human body
and turns it first to a monster bubbling in pain,
then finally to a blank, viscid, and implacable enemy:
image of the human self-experiment. Or rather, this image
as it appears to the hucksters who made these awful movies
and sold them to my nights, otherwise quiet in the hum
of refrigerator engine and whistle of aural nerves decaying.
I wondered why I didn't turn them off and think of you,
didn't pierce through fear of the great strain it would be
to compose my mind's noise, my senses' palsy
the way hands can be folded or legs formed into a root,
the sort of root a canoe's hull or the belly of a tern
offers to water, moving on its own pressure and soft shadow.
Was I hopeless because you were never thinking of me?
But you didn't yet exist then, when I was sitting in my kitchen,
hoping soon to turn off the companionable horror of my day
and think of you, quiet, powerful, come from the future
rescuing me not as I imagined you but as you will be.

The Sun

My sun, I see your colour fall
again on everything on earth. The trees
are lifted out of darkness,
and there are flowers,
people (they talk), and houses that create
warm spaces in the great
night and the cold, waiting for you,
almost in despair, their powers
fading. These all spring up
from dimness to full life again
because of you, as if they were no more
than low reliefs carved badly in black slate
until you shine. Then their true bodies
open as desert plants
rise when rare rainfall brings to sudden birth
brief spring, insane and joyful:
plants that break only once through covering earth,
as if young men and women opened
flat gravestones, and walked out
by the same entranceway the terrifying corpses
yesterday and years ago
went in.

Acknowledgements

Thanks to the editors of the following publications, in which the poems in *The Sentinel* first appeared, some in earlier versions and under other titles:

Books in Canada: "Return to the Fountain"
Canadian Literature: "Two Crickets"
The Drunken Boat: "Dandelion," "Mastectomy"
Event: "The Butterfly"
Exile: The Literary Quarterly: "Final Flower," "Poem of Courtly Love," "Ideal Song of the Communists"
The Fiddlehead: "The Ant," "The Source," "The Sun He Said"
The Gettysburg Review: "Kurt Mazur's Ears"
Grain: "Zoo Keeper"
The I.V. Lounge Reader (anthology; ed. Paul Vermeersch): "To the Still Unborn"
The Malahat Review: "Old Pet"
The New Quarterly: "Arrogance," "In a Prosperous Country"
Poetry (Chicago): "At Two Solemn Musicks," "Better Days," "Busman's Honeymoon," "Cleanliness," "The Jar," "Place," "Pleasure Cruiser," "The Seer," "The Sentinel," "Sound of Hungry Animals," "The

Tidal Wave," "Tragic Vision and Beyond," "Your Story," "You That
   I Loved," "What Way," "What We Had"
Seeds: "The Light"
The Shore: "The Moment"
The Southwest Review: "Vermin; or, Weariness," "Warren"
Third Floor Lounge (anthology; ed. Jeramy Dodds): "The *Titanic*"
The Walrus: "Her Work"
The Yale Review: "The First, Second, Third, and Fourth"

Some of the above poems were reprinted, and other poems in *The
Sentinel* appeared for the first time, in limited edition chapbooks:

Crossroads Near Somewhere (Windsor, ON: Biblioasis, 2005); thanks
   to editor and publisher Dan Wells
Now That You Revive (Victoria, BC: Frog Hollow Press, 2007); thanks
   to publisher Caryl Peters and editor Shane Nielson; Frog Hollow
   Press also published *Cassandra* as a limited edition broadside
Sound of Hungry Animals (Toronto, London, Dublin: Rufus Books,
   2007); thanks to editor and publisher Agnes Cserhati

"The Sentinel" received the 2005 Bess Hokin Prize from *Poetry*, and
"Vermin; or, Weariness" received the 2005 Elizabeth Matchett Stover
Award from *The Southwest Review*. *Poetry Daily* (the website) selected
"Tragic Vision and Beyond" (from *Poetry*), "The First, Second, Third,
and Fourth" (from *The Yale Review*), and "What Way" (from *Poetry*)
for feature presentation in November 2003, January 2005, and July
2006 respectively.

Special thanks to Ken Babstock, poet, friend, and my editor on this
book, for contributions to the choice, arrangement, music, and sense
of the poems.

About the Author

A. F. Moritz has written fifteen books of poetry, and has received the Guggenheim Fellowship, the Award in Literature of the American Academy and Institute of Arts and Letters, and the Ingram Merrill Fellowship. His collection, *Night Street Repairs,* won the ReLit Award and, most recently, *The Sentinel* won the 2009 Griffin Poetry Prize, was a finalist for the Governor General's Literary Award, and was a *Globe and Mail* Top 100 Book. Moritz lives in Toronto and teaches at Victoria College, University of Toronto.